THE WHOLE SINGING OCEAN

The Whole Singing Ocean

JESSICA MOORE

NIGHTWOOD EDITIONS | 2020

Nightwood Editions
P.O. Box 1779
Gibsons, BC VON 1V0
Canada
www.nightwoodeditions.com

COVER DESIGN: Angela Yen
TYPOGRAPHY: Carleton Wilson
COVER IMAGE: Original linocut by Jessica Moore

Nightwood Editions acknowledges the support of the Canada Council for the Arts, the Government of Canada, and the Province of British Columbia through the BC Arts Council.

This book has been produced on 100% post-consumer recycled, ancient-forest-free paper, processed chlorine-free and printed with vegetable-based dyes.

Printed and bound in Canada.

LIBRARY AND ARCHIVES CANADA CATALOGUING IN PUBLICATION

Title: The whole singing ocean / by Jessica Moore.
Names: Moore, Jessica, 1978- author.
Description: A story in poetic fragments.
Identifiers: Canadiana (print) 20200213792 | Canadiana (ebook) 20200213806 |
  ISBN 9780889713789 (softcover) | ISBN 9780889713796 (ebook)
Classification: LCC PS8626.O5939 W56 2020 | DDC C811/.6—dc23

for my mother, Angela Moore

& for the boat builder

Contents

The whale　11

Warning shot across the bow　26

Lines go blurry　45

L'École en bateau (The Boat School)　55

Can you keep a secret?　56

Foucault, or silence the surest fetters　68

Flotsam & jetsam　76

The beginning—no, further back　87

In his own words　91

The language of transgression　97

Groundswell　103

The shores of the world　107

I have a room in the dark　116

Other voices　134

The key that never fits any lock　138

Un séjour de rupture　146

The organ on the porch　154

Neither of us hungered　158

The whole singing ocean　160

Notes　186

Acknowledgements　190

About the Author　192

But the one thing we dread
o keep clear of his eye

– Coast of Peru, folk song

What haunts you wants a form that is like none other

– Phil Hall

The whale

The dreams began when I was still a child

    always from shore always racing to see them

leaping dark joy in waves
hurled through with light

—

so when the boat builder invited me onto his boat
and told me his story
I listened

We were lying side by side in the hull
The sea was calm but stirred

bubbles sounding along the wood
like the whir in a vast aquarium

and there we were, specks
inside

Long before
building his own boat

he'd apprenticed aboard
a marine biology vessel

Being the youngest
he was chosen to be towed behind

diving mask on
eye out for them

If he saw one, he was to tug the rope as a signal

And me—
many nights I dreamed

Awe was in every dream & sometimes
it was the kind that makes the hackles rise up
& sometimes it was the kind that opens wings

~

This day he'd been trawling along thinking of music, jazz
the near impossibility of true improvisation, real randomness
because how can you trick yourself into playing something new?

Patterns pull us, patterns form us
form our slow sleeping states
our waking ones too

unless we keep
wildly alert
on the lookout—

That summer I'd thrown myself
to the lions of another adventure

~

Curled facing each other I confess I'd wished on the ferry crossing
to spot one—seeing a whale was a fathomless want

the kind you carry
in childhood

Once in Newfoundland I'd boarded
the whale-watching boat and then—

nothing—
only the dismal puffins on their shit-covered rock

Fog so thick
I could have choked

I burst into sobs inside the car
slammed my hands against the dash

His hands and mine between us
though we have both been inside
a greater love, a greater grief

Still it's comfort

In the presence of something far more vast than ourselves

—

ANOTHER BOAT BUILDER EH yeah this one's a real charmer, musician and all, never stops talking DID HE OFFER TO BUY YOU LUNCH no nothing like that we simply struck a chord or rather two chords side by side ON THE ORGAN yeah the one on the porch WOULD'VE THOUGHT IT WOULD BE MOSS-COVERED BY NOW 'cause of all the rain YES the blackberries were threatening to cover the high E but we never got that far anyway decided to have a Bloody Mary at the bar BAR FULL O' BOAT BUILDERS there are a lot of them in these parts WHAT ABOUT YOU GOT YOUR SEA LEGS funny you should say that we were just talking about it the other night AND it's not so much sea legs as sea ears COME AGAIN throws my inner ear equilibrium right off

I still said I'd sleep over on his boat

There is a lot we carry with us
into the hulls of ships

~

And I remember a thousand times
believing the dark was good

descending to meet it like trees to their roots

and I remember a thousand times
believing that it was not

Sometimes night is the surest thing there is

After the whale-watching boat
I took the coastal road

down the peninsula, following a hunch
parked the car past a narrow causeway

When I'd been walking the mist-pinned beach
no longer than twenty minutes, the fog lifted

revealing the fins of them, tens of them
just metres offshore

So close I could hear it:
the breath of whales

—

And on this day (he tells me) he did see one
a mother humpback
looming up from the depths beneath

He reached for the rope overhead
and here is where the story goes slant—

remember the tale of the mouse and the whale NOT SURE I KNOW THAT ONE you do I'm sure you do—one of those tear-jerking kids' books TELL IT TO ME AGAIN the mouse is all alone in the immensity of the sea YES alone and thinking of what it means to be a speck in all that vastness BIT OF A PHILOSOPHER, THAT MOUSE feeling alone and insignificant AS WE ALL ARE WONT TO DO SOMETIMES and then his boat capsizes and he's full of fear YES but the whale comes to save him YES. I REMEMBER IT NOW

—

Have you ever lain
on the surface of the water
and felt the pull?

In the midst of all the wondering
the awe-filledness and triumph and what-have-you
there was something more about whales
a kind of *noblesse, a mélancolie*

WHAT IS IT WITH ALL THE FRENCH WORDS ANYWAY ha,
pourquoi, do you find them off-putting THAT'S NOT THE WORD
I WOULD HAVE CHOSEN *orgueilleux* then WHAT DOES THAT
MEAN it means prideful and perhaps condescending YOU SAID IT
NOT ME sometimes they just fit better, like music. I think if the boat
builder could, he would rather speak in riffs much of the time BACK
TO HIM ARE WE or like going into someone else's workshop and
seeing a tool that would fit the job just right—like using a drawknife on
a boat instead of a planer LISTEN TO YOU—YOU THINKING OF
BECOMING A BOAT BUILDER NOW TOO no, but I have done
my share of listening to *them*—that last time we stayed up all night 'til
the phosphorescence dimmed

gravity and a deeper blue
the many-layered thing

DID YOU KNOW THAT PHOSPHORESCENCES ARE LIKE
PLANKTON AND THEIR BRILLIANCE IS INVOLUNTARY all I
know is that it felt like we were suspended in a sky full of stars

and there is, too, the cold white moon

DID YOU KNOW THAT FEELING OF SUSPENSION IS REGULATED BY THE INNER EAR sometimes I'd rather not know all the answers PEOPLE WHO DESIGN FUNPARK RIDES STUDY UP ON IT sometimes I'd rather just sit back in the not-knowing

> and further still is swirling dark
> as though whales may rise straight out
> of the void—that great mystery

IF MYSTERY IS SIMPLY WHAT WE CANNOT SEE THEN THE OCEAN WOULD BE PARTICULARLY RICH and what about the nighttime ocean

In the moment when he reached overhead
his instinct was not to tug on the rope, not to signal
but to locate the metal of the clasp
and release it—

Where a French word might be useful
you find yourself face down in water with pewter
skies pressing low (*grisaille*) and the long low ocean
pressing back (*miroitant*), showing the sky its own
face and gleaming, the thrum-rumble of slow motor
pulling you along by a rope

eye on the depths

each inch of your narrow body
sleeked inside wetsuit except for face and hands
each metre of water baleened
and if you see one
reach overhead, tug the rope
signal to the mate on board so he'll call out to the captain

Except for the rumble it's quiet
and in spite of the forward combing there's stillness—
you are moving still through vastest grey
thoughts careening to Django's guitar
water-cold fingers feeling out jazz chords
'til there sings out

a new sound

brief, but for that moment—all—

coming at you all-sided all-filling and you see her
rising like an arpeggio from the dark

Then there are no thoughts

Overhead your hand clambers
and reaching the rope rather than tugging
you unclip. Swim free

Unlinked now to the human world you dive
down toward the fins, the dark and gleaming

body, the broadly turning being
filling up your view; you glide

lungs pounding, until
you find the eye

You have never seen an eye such as this, so large
asking nothing—

and then there you are
just you and the whale

With her you are the vast mirroring sea. You are
the whole singing ocean. You are beheld
held in that eye and you

are whole

≈

Warning shot across the bow

And look! look! look! I think those little fish
better wake up...
—Mary Oliver

Years—I mean years—later, I was driving up highway 101
and when I got to San Francisco
I stopped in to see the boat builder

He lived in a northern suburb now
with his wife and baby

—

WHAT EVER HAPPENED WITH YOU TWO ANYWAY oh, it's
not really about that, though OKAY, ARTFUL DODGER he had
something I wanted, something like a key WHAT ABOUT FOR
HIM when you live on a small island, and you have a story to tell, fresh
ears are always welcome I suppose GUESS IT DOESN'T HURT IF
A PRETTY FACE COMES ALONG WITH THEM and afterwards
there's always a tenderness

SO YOU ROLLED UP AFTER ALL THIS TIME wait though—first
an echo of another kind, for I'd longed to see the redwoods. It was a
dogged want, the kind you carry in childhood, and on that trip it felt like
I was always racing the sunset BTW IT'S A DOCUMENTED FACT
THAT PEOPLE IN OLD FOLKS' HOMES GET ALL ANTSY JUST
BEFORE SUNSET—HOT & BOTHERED AND RESTLESS—so
there I was at Muir Woods half an hour before said sunset, and I wanted
more than just to see them, I wanted to walk among their grace until I
felt something change. I wanted to live among their silent grace until I
felt my hard edges go, until I became—like them ALWAYS SEEKING

RAPTURE well… ALWAYS WITH THAT SUNSET FEELING.
SO YOU ROLLED UP… yes, down a smooth cul-de-sac into their
driveway

~

He had a wide and easy smile
like before but I didn't remember him
being such a nurturer, stirring pots
on the stove, asking after the boat builders at home

once we were all sitting down to dinner, I told him I'd been writing
about that moment with the whale HE MUST'VE BEEN CHUFFED
his eyebrows went right up into the creases on his forehead, growing
taller as the hairline skulked away, lines clean and even like the planks
OH NO DON'T SAY IT on a boat *GROAN*

~

"Really?" said the boat builder, the corners of his mouth loose and
grinning, and his eyes went here and there as though searching for the
reason I might have done such a thing, or combing memory to find the
night when he had told it to me

~

a night when I felt myself as flint, no pause between the world and
me—ALWAYS SEEKING RAPTURE—and something perfect—

…perfectly still, and deep
as I imagine the ocean that day

And even though I know the story to be set
in warm island waters it is a steel
grisaille I see, not like the dark deep blue
of the bay in the Pacific
where I lay with him in the hull, falling

not for the man, but the story

My life's work, laying down in boats
or under stars
or hundreds-of-years-old rooftops
or tent canvas or my own known ceiling

collecting the tales

⸺

"I've been thinking about that time a lot myself," he says.

Something in me closes up at the same time that something else shifts
forward, curious, digging. I have carried
his story for so long, and the way his face has changed—
almost apologetic, looking side to side and then at me—
makes me freeze.

"All the articles are in French. I've been waiting for a translator."

SO WHAT WAS THE STORY oh it was awful—like something you've
held as beautiful for years has just been peeled back to reveal—WHAT
HAPPENED and that's just me speaking—imagine what it was like for
him who actually lived it WHAT HAPPENED there's such a particular
violence to the kind of rearranging you have to do JUST SPIT IT OUT,
WOULD YA

~

He fleshes out a scene I never
remember hearing before
not a marine biology vessel, after all, and not just a boat

but rather a French travelling school, of sorts
whose base at the time was a shipwreck
miles from anywhere

The Silver Bank, haven for sea mammals. Where the great
Atlantic trench rises to a mere forty feet deep
Where the whales migrate every year—

They anchored and occupied the end of the wreck
not submerged, read and studied and slept there. Cooked bread
in the old galley stove, knee-deep

in water. It sounds jagged. Rusting and
dangerous. The kids cooked, cleaned, kept ship,
kept lookout. Their limbs

were tanned and muscled and the water
was bleached turquoise
lightening to white

coral underneath, deceptive
smoothness. Those cuts
are the worst kind

He was there for five months—he was not
the youngest, and with only grade school French
he was not inside the inner circle—

lucky

—

I'M STARTING TO GET THAT MURKY FEELING would you like
some ginger tea, I've just put a pot on the stove I SAID MURKY NOT
QUEASY BUT OKAY I WON'T SAY NO

The boat builder's eyes on his hands, eyebrows alternating
between rising up into lines and angling down
fishing rods in the water off the wreck

wreck of a boat populated by beautiful, tanned
children who run this little world

His own son, sixteen months old, whimpers
in his mother's arms, then smiles
across the table, a study in contradictions

"I never saw it," says the boat builder. "It never happened to me."

—

WHY DID YOU STOP I don't know, it's so much, there's just so much,
it feels familiar somehow, I don't know where to begin

Begin with the road that leads
from the organ on the porch
to the bay, the road where
you saw a snake once
and the snake was the whole
infinite line of what links you to the living

Begin with that road
There are blackberries there
in August, in the shade

They said, years later, of the children they had been—nine to fifteen years old—that they didn't want to disappoint Léo

—

Léonide Kameneff. Seventy-eight. (Then, fifty-six). Captain of the *Karrek Ven*, an antique sailing ship built in Brittany, the ship that carried, over the course of twelve years, four hundred pubescent boys and sixty girls to the shipwreck, the Polyxeni, in the Azores islands. Former child psychologist, Foucault enthusiast, desirous of developing a system and a forum (read: *logic*) to abolish the separation between adults and children.

last night at the bar with H., my friend from Berlin, we were talking about how quietly subtly and completely we can be swallowed up by the atmosphere that surrounds us, so silently we are unawares, so penetratingly we can become a link or a cog or however you want to say it of that logic LIKE ASKING A FISH, *HOW'S THE WATER?* LOGIC IS A GOOD WORD

the bartender said she told her psychiatrist once that if she had lived in Nazi Germany—or any fascist regime—she thinks she might have gone along with it, like she might not have even known, or had the wherewithal to do otherwise EGAD, WHAT A QUESTION. WE MUST ALL HAVE ASKED IT AT SOME POINT the murk of doubt, where within oneself the conviction would come from, in the face of this quiet killing sureness WELL OF COURSE THIS MAKES ME THINK OF THE OCEANS... the oceans THE ISLANDS IN THE OCEAN which ones THE KILLING ONES, THE ISLANDS OF PLASTIC oh, geez. but what is the link to logic WELL JUST THE NUMBNESS. YOU BUY PLASTIC DON'T YOU, I KNOW BECAUSE I'VE SEEN YOU WITH YOUR LITTLE PACKAGES OF NUTS, LIKE A NIHILISTIC LITTLE SQUIRREL IN A FUTURE, WHICH IS NOW, LITTERED WITH ALL OUR INSIDIOUS KILLING LOGIC

The children were rulers, were golden
removed from every signpost, every *repère*
and from there they could see wild storms
roll in, and from there they could see humpbacks swim
and from there they could see the dark
movements of the moon, and of transparent overlapping selves

They were creating a new world

"I thought I was free," said one

⁓

NOTHING IS SHARP. NOTHING IS BLACK AND WHITE God,
some things are, they have to be

⁓

Said Foucault: *Don't ask me who I am, or tell me to stay the same.*

⁓

Bernard Poggi, fifty-nine. Himself a victim of Kameneff at the age of
twelve.

IT'S PAST MURKY, AND EVEN QUEASY I know, let's talk about
the wind for a while

—

There is a wind system called the Nortada, caused by the anticyclone
of the Azores. During periods of the Nortada, the warmer top layers of
water are pushed out to the open, and cold swaths from deep down take
their place. This means the top layer of the ocean becomes unusually
nutrient-rich. This means constant movement. This means frequent
fogs.

And fog does just what it's always done.

—

The Azores, last
vestige of sooty-winged puffins
(so they were there, too)
nests among the honey stone
nests among the calendula
In French the flower is called *souci*
which also means trouble
or worry

—

WHAT DID FOUCAULT SAY ABOUT THE BOUNDARIES BE-
TWEEN ADULTS AND CHILDREN? I'm not clear on that part yet

Someone in their testimony called the wreck the perfect trap

—

Cast out of the garden

zebra fish sea fans jellyfish urchins
yellow purple blazing garden
fronds waving secret rhythms
moray eels, coral, whales—

childhood

—

The victims said it was *une rupture psychologique.* Do they mean in the sense of a separation from what came before, or a breaking apart? I can't tell in translation, but what is clear is that they were inculcated into a space entirely separate from their lives before.

Kameneff justified himself through Foucault. He was an educated man.

ON THE SUBJECT OF WHALES—IT HAS BEEN SUGGESTED THAT WHALES ARE ACTUALLY THE MANIFESTATION OF DOLPHINS' HIGHER SELVES "it has been suggested"? where are you getting your information I HAVE MY SOURCES but how reliable are they WELL, THESE ONES MAY HAVE BEEN *AHEM* AN ALIEN... hm? come again *SIGH* AN ALIEN CONSCIOUSNESS I see, and where did you come across this alien consciousness OH YOU KNOW, YOU WANDER, YOU STROLL THROUGH THE PARK AT NIGHT, YOU NEVER KNOW WHO YOU'RE GOING TO MEET you mean you found it on the internet YES

if whales are dolphins' higher selves, does that mean there are humanoid giants wandering around somewhere that are *our* higher selves? IT DOESN'T WORK LIKE THAT okay... BECAUSE OF GRAVITY... what does gravity have to do with it? IT'S JUST NOT THE BEST—IT DOESN'T PROVIDE THE IDEAL CIRCUMSTANCES FOR MANIFESTATION OF SOMETHING HIGHER, WHEREAS THE BUOYANCY OF THE SEA... I suppose I should know by now not to look for reason I BEG TO DIFFER, I BELIEVE I AM GENERALLY VERY GIVEN TO REASON I suppose this area allows for something outside of logic? AH, THERE'S THAT WORD AGAIN

At seventy-six he is a haunted man with hooded eyes
but maybe everyone accused of a hideous crime
looks this way.

Cuisiner. The judge said *cuisiner.* "I've never been put through the wringer like that" (only in French the word is *cooked*), said Kameneff after the first day of trial, and the judge said, "Well then we will continue to put you through it."

SO I'VE BEEN READING ABOUT FOUCAULT SINCE YOU
MENTIONED HIM and, what have you found? MOSTLY JUST
THAT HE WAS A SLIPPERY SUCKER—SCHOLARS TEND
TO WIND AROUND THINGS WHEN THEY SPEAK OF HIM,
THEY HAVE TROUBLE PINNING HIM DOWN

—

Pin him
lynch pin
kingpin
kingfisher

If there are cormorants
are they mostly in the mornings?
If there are mornings are they moored
to kingfishers? If there are no moorings
is the boat, the hurt, real?

The hurt is always real

Seabirds filled with
trash. Plastic. Debris.
Caps and lighters and tampon applicators.
Industrial packing beads, the new
sand of the sea

Look at all they carry inside

—

SEEMS TO ME FOUCAULT JUST WANTED TO TAKE EVERY
GODDAMN THING APART. TO GET TO THE ROOT OF
THINGS AND THEN BLAST EVEN THE ROOT. MORE
INTERESTED IN UNDOING THAN IN CREATING ANY
SHELTER but where did he find refuge?

EVERY INSTANCE OF POWER AND POWER RELATIONS,
EVERY BOUNDARY, WAS A THING TO BE BUSTED UP sliced
open with exactos and all the contents spread out over the beach

Anything can be the trigger
backward down a binding path

One man from the wreck named
the smell of nutmeg, limes

The whole world becomes
perilous

We don't speak of so many things
as though by keeping quiet we keep

ourselves safe
(Ourselves, or them?)

A few brave or tired ones came forward
tired of dragging this quiet thing

around with them, tired of fighting
the slippery path in the middle of love

in the middle of the kitchen
rife with citrus

Green rinds wrung dry beside the knife

BIRDS ARE ONE THING

kingpin
lynch pin
kingfisher

BUT GOD, WHALES TOO?

roll in
whole hymn
holy

CUT OPEN TO REVEAL—
AFTER GHASTLY DEATHS—
what did that scientist call them?
FLOATING TOXIC DUMPS

Foolhardy to think anything is
Separate

—

From the top of the mast the sea
was a jewel, green

soft and stroking and numinous
buttressing mysticism

From up there you might
look and ask, lucid, am I dreaming

receiving no answer
desiring no answer

Come evening, the sea shows a bluer face
still and smooth, and I think of Cézanne
how closely he leaned in

Painting the same mountain, again
& again & again
coming to know it like a child
or a lover

not both

≈

Lines go blurry

I was at the art gallery the other day with H.—she had just had her heart broken again and so was extra perceptive... the Turner exhibit TURNER WAS AHEAD OF HIS TIME most of the paintings so mild, sluggish pastel sunsets—but there was one that grasped me and would not let go, it hung all by itself on a dark-grey wall and the sea foamed and furied and I stared down a round column straight into the heart of the storm

THE STORY IS THAT TURNER HAD HIMSELF LASHED TO THE MAST FOR THAT ONE wow! HE TOLD THEM NOT TO UNTIE HIM NO MATTER HOW MUCH HE PLEADED wait... NO MATTER HOW LOUD HIS CRIES GOT HE TOLD THEM TO LEAVE HIM THERE ...I think you're mixing him up... JUST BLOCK YOUR EARS AGAINST MY CRIES, HE COMMANDED you're talking about Odysseus, aren't you OH RIGHT

Odysseus and the Sirens, the beguiling, the aching pull, the longing for something just out of reach HERE WE GO, SHE'S WAXING RAPTUROUS AGAIN, SOMEONE GET ME SOME OILCLOTH TO STUFF IN MY EARS alright, alright

On the opposite wall there was a projection showing different views of the sea, videos of waves, mountains of them. My friend, shining today in that way the shattered do, said, "Just think—this is what Turner would have had to paint from. The moving water. There were no photographs then." Crests of waves lifted, a split second at a time, everything lifting and sinking and endless. No still point to paint from

He had to become the still point

"I never saw it," said the boat builder,
"it never happened to me."

He said that back in the fall.
But then, last month, I talked to him again.

⁓

This story unfolding at the rate that I write
Each of us—story, boat builder, me—just keeping up
No that's not true. The story has no effort
The story has no imperative
(Or does it?)

This last time we spoke, he pulled the car over
toothy child in the back seat smiling
both their faces through the tiny angles
of the phone screen, and he told me more scraps
gulls screaming

Am I vulturous? What is it that compels me?

Try not to seem too hungry

Lines go blurry. Story swerves

And then you have to
sidle up to it, just like a scared
animal don't

look it in the eye

—

I have more questions than clarity right now WELL QUESTIONS'LL
GET YOU SOMEWHERE—THAT'S WHAT FOUCAULT
WOULD SAY, ANYWAY still don't know what to do with him, and
now I'm having a déjà vu HERE HAVE A BEER AND THEN IT
WILL BE A DÉJÀ BU

(Interlude)

so I have a question I'd rather not ask… I've been thinking about you MY EARS WERE BURNING we've got that bond haven't we LIKE TWO SCALLOPS IN A SHELL I don't feel a need to pin you down THAT'S PROBABLY WHY THIS HAS LASTED SO LONG (YOU KNOW HOW SQUIRRELLY I GET) I don't feel a need, but it seems like the whole thing is a bit confusing to the readers, so how do we explain it to them? WELL WE'VE KNOWN EACH OTHER A LONG TIME yes INSIDE AND OUT, YOU MIGHT SAY that's clever I WOULDN'T EXACTLY SAY WE SEE EYE TO EYE— WE'RE LIKE APPLES AND ORANGES MOST OF THE TIME are we? BUT WE'RE COMFORTABLE AS AN OLD SHOE, AND, WELL—I LIKE THE CUT OF YOUR JIB I don't know if they'll accept that

—

are you only inside my head? CAN YOU JUST LET ME BE WHAT I AM? THERE ARE THINGS I KNOW THAT YOU DON'T KNOW YET you're either in or you're out SOME DO SOME DON'T, BUD

The boat builder tells me about his arrival to the *École en bateau*.

"It was my first time in a plane and I was alone. Some boys my age met me at the dock. They didn't speak English. We motored the small green-and-white skiff to the *Karrek Ven*, which was everything I had imagined, white topsides and dark-green bulwarks, a raw salt-stained deck and rich-red tanbark sails.

"I was now a child of the sea," he says.

Below deck, Prokofiev was playing, and now every time he hears *Montagues and Capulets*, bam, he's back.

The crew—the children—were leaning
over books and papers. It was 1990—the captain sat
typing on a cutting-edge Commodore 64.
Peering over the rims of his glasses he said gravely,
"Welcome, my young friend, to your great adventure."

That first night the boat builder dove with the other children from the prow.

"The crew swam naked but I was shy."

—

"I learned to eat liver, cow's tongue, pig's feet.
Every night we sipped hot cocoa thickened with cornstarch—
that taste is forever embedded in my memory.

"There were no sleeping quarters for the kids.
Léo and Bernard had their berths and the rest of us laid out bedrolls
wherever we found room. Some slept on deck under the stars
among the sail bags. The net below the bowsprit was the best."

"I never saw it. It never happened to me."
He meant the worst of it.
He was spared the worst.

~

The boat builder saw the odd
requirements and thought this must
be just how they do it in Europe

Standing under the outdoor shower
an older boy's hands on you

~

I wonder now if language
was part of what saved him from worse

the distance between English and French
like the sound of a far-off hammer across the bay

He ducked his head at all this nakedness
didn't want one bit to take off his shorts

but then they'd reach some marvellous site
and he'd be told to stay behind

Finally one day another boy told him it would be better if he did
tu devrais laisser le soleil te caresser le vent t'embrasser

That first time oh the awkwardness
of limbs. That first time oh the length of limbs
but none long enough to hide behind

~

Symphonies, dolphins, archaeology, islands,
he packed up that perfect time in boxes even his wife
knew nothing about, stuffed them into the coach house

now he knows
it was no perfect time. Still—

    the freedom—

~

I have stood at the edges of the earth and wanted
to go just a little further where I might catch
the rapture racketing past

He has been to the ends of the earth and how
could he now be content with the crummy suburbs
the Subways and Walmarts, a piña colada at Chili's
the most cosmopolitan thing around?

He has sailed a boat across the world—

An early taste of adventure can wreck you for life

—

Down below, five boys gather
summoned in a circle by one man

This boy's hands are awkward, his eyes
awkward, his face. Every part of his body
he can possibly turn, he turns away
without breaking rank

The boys don't look at each other
The man looks at all of them

≈

I: I'm following you, I'm trying anyway, sorry about the times when I try to take the lead

Story: Only one of us can lead

I: I was never any good at ballroom

Story: I'm like the sea you know

I: I was afraid in the night and it seemed to me the ghost was water

Story: What could water possibly want from you

I: That's just it. It is neither caring nor desiring and that in itself can be fearsome

Story: You think water does not hunger?

I: ...

Story: Remember: what haunts you wants a form that is like none other

L'École en bateau (The Boat School)

Established in 1969, it was said to be inspired by the same ideals that led to the May 1968 uprising in France where students, and then later, workers, demanded dramatic changes to the status quo in the form of cultural, political and sexual revolution. It was an alternative to contemporary school, providing a hands-on learning experience where children between the ages of nine and sixteen spent a few months to a few years travelling throughout the Mediterranean and later across the Atlantic, with the goal of developing life skills through practical experience rather than through studying theory. A fundamental goal was to abolish barriers between children and adults. To that end, the children became the ship's crew, with responsibility for upkeep, maintenance and food preparation throughout the voyage. During the thirty-three years *L'École en bateau* operated, more than four hundred boys and sixty girls left their families for extended periods of time, for what they must have imagined would be an idyllic existence, the opportunity of a lifetime.

The first public hint of trouble occurred in 1971 when a student lodged a complaint of abuse against the founder, former child psychotherapist Léonide Kameneff. More serious trouble became evident in 1994 when the first accusations of rape were made against Kameneff by former pupils. The school closed in 2000. After years of legal challenges and more than thirty public complaints, in 2013 he and two of his former staff were convicted of rape and sexual abuse of minors.

–Angela Moore

Can you keep a secret?

The boat builder sends me a link
to the documentary, filmed
at the time of the court case

⁓

A wall of glass. This is how one man describes it
He used to be on the other side, among
the living

That's what it does. Seals you off
Splintering clear
and sudden—

or slow, the frog's skin
in scalding water

⁓

Aboard the *École en bateau,* Léo presides
over the dinner table, mocks
the new boy from Canada who doesn't know how
to cook pasta, al dente. Everyone laughs

Power of whittling people down

We know how birds murmur
and we know how whales sing

we know how air turns to glass
when death or a hand transgresses

we know the *décalage*
of a far-off hammer

sound hitting
two beats after the swing

we know the cringe-turned-pulp
inside

when cut down by the king
at the head of the table

or when something different appears
in the shape of someone you know

Léo would say, under cover of dark, in their bunks,
"If it feels good, it can't be hurting you.

"Right?"

~

End-of-day sessions
in the dark of the hold

A candle flame leans left, then right
mountains in the sea

All the children around the table
All urged to take each other down

They were discouraged from writing home too often
How could their parents

—landlocked, conventional, a thousand miles away—
possibly understand?

~

the boat builder grew up a boy in the suburbs but you know how it is,
the sea calls OH I KNOW THE CALL BUD

He mails me a novel written by one of the other kids from the boat. Someone he called a friend. It's titled *Les perles de lumière*.

"I can't read it," he says. "I hardly remember three words of French. So you might as well take it and tell me what he says."

Though it's based partly on what happened, it has the remove of fiction. Which is a little like a pearl. One true hard thing at the centre.

—

I sit down with the book and Oliver Schroer
the sun of that music the wind in your face

I read about the morning one boy put on Fauré's requiem

heavy first bars falling chords
everyone's eyes sliding sideways
ça va pas
pas comme ça qu'on commence le matin

Always something to get wrong
for all the freewheeling ideals
there were a lot of rules

and every sign pointed toward

one
man's
logic

Most all the books on board were from Ancient Greece
all the records classical

Oh those Greeks & their unflappable
sexuality

courtyards of boys
passing
        grapes
tongue to tongue

All signs, one logic, and if something intervened—
someone's cassette tape of David Bowie—

it was crushed under the heel like a mollusc

⁓

That same afternoon they dove from the deck
turquoise-white flashing water of the cove

arced themselves above the surface
lay back to receive the sky and all its blue

remembering what they learned of Saussure's cyanometer
& other marvellous measuring tools

THE *AHEM* ALIEN CONSCIOUSNESS ALSO SPOKE OF THE
IMPORTANCE OF PLAY. THIS IS WHAT IT WANTS US TO
REMEMBER, THROUGH THE DOLPHINS and you found this
where, again? oh yes, the internet, that other rich and toxic sea

⁓

That afternoon there was the devil to pay
for frittering away the time
Léo didn't believe in play

⁓

I keep reading, sifting
through the distance of fiction
& the other language

I've been told I speak French as though I'm walking on tiptoe
holding up the edges of my dress

In the novel, two boys sit on deck for the night watch
bowlful of stars above
cradle of dark all around

A wave sweeps over the bridge and three flying fish
fall to the deck. "Thank goodness," says one
"I never want to see another banana"

They learned to climb like bears, hugging
the trunks and lunging for the loot. One day
four proud boys brought back a boatload of green

bunches so big
they threatened
to topple them

& then seven days without wind
just the heat and the endless banana everything
when the fruit ripened all at once

banana compote
banana purée
banana crêpes
banana flambé

Thick sugar sick in their mouths

Return to that summer, to the hull of his boat
Now your limbs again. Now his limbs. Lines blurred
but not crossed

—

Now he'll curve the crescent of himself
against your back and only sleep
will make him stop talking

Take a float plane in the morning and from up there
see the bay shining like an eye

—

I needed to hear the story of the whale that summer
like I needed to swim in luminous green ribbons

The man I loved had died. That's not what this is about
I've carried and written that story already
Still, it's everywhere

I needed to hear the story of the whale then, whole
inviolate. No before or after. I needed to remember
there were eyes that large and wise, asking nothing

Each time I talk to the boat builder, something else is revealed. Remember how I said he was on board for five months YEAH well I got that wrong—it was a year and a half HOLY HANNAH

And the shipwreck was in the Caribbean, not the Azores (though the *Karrek Ven* did go there, too)

The part about him being the youngest, too—of course he wasn't, he was fifteen—*an uncool, late-blooming tenth grader*
Strange how memory is a creature of its own and strong-willed

Or—you might say—flighty, untethered

~

Some of them were only nine when they began

~

I write the boat builder a letter.

Dear A.,

Here I am back in Montreal, in my 3½ on the top floor (my white tower) where the white skies and gulls crying make it feel like the sea. How's the heart, you ask—and I think of the beam of the lighthouse, from V. Woolf's novel. It's always there signalling something. But it's on the outside. Seems I'm always searching for something just out of reach.

I found a labyrinth the other day in the most unlikely of places: deep in the financial district, tucked between skyscrapers. A surprising oasis.

I'm making it a ritual to go there a few times a month with the story in mind.

Thanks for the book. There is a character named A., did you know that? I guess that's you … botching the pasta, staying up on night watch when flying fish landed on deck. Do you remember any of that? There has been no mention yet, a third of the way in, of what happened except to say that the man dreaming the dreams—an old man now—lives behind a wall of glass.

⁓

A year and a half. That will change you. At fifteen, a whole sagittal slice of life.

⁓

Can people be broken?

Can they be made whole again?

≈

I: What about you? what do you want?

Story: I already said I'm like the sea. And the sea is only ever always endlessly being and being and being and all your strength is nothing against it, as you've well learned.

I: Can you keep a secret?

Story: All of them. I can keep them all.

Foucault, or silence the surest fetters

I lie on the grass with Foucault
I feel myself stirred

*Thus the image of the imperial prude is emblazoned
on our restrained, mute, and hypocritical society.*
(and this is just the beginning)

What prudishness
do I inherit?

The seventeenth century, *a time of direct gestures,
shameless discourse, and open transgressions,
when anatomies were shown and intermingled at will,
and knowing children hung about amid the laughter of adults...*

Go on break free

—

YOU COULD TAKE HIS WORDS AND JUSTIFY WHATEVER
YOU WANTED

They call him the philosopher of power

but he refused to define it
Not like other philosophers
who allow themselves to be distilled
down to an essence

one pure potent beloved
concept

~

LIKE I SAID, A SLIPPERY SUCKER. I'M GETTING A
HANKERING FOR THE SURENESS OF PLATO'S FORMS.
OR TOURNIER'S CAVE—THAT SMOOTH WOMB WHERE
ROBINSON HID FROM THE WORLD but everyone knows the
future is dark, & everything alive is always changing—

isn't that the thrill?

~

Listen up, said the young Foucault, but no one paid him any mind. So
he showed up to class dressed as a motorcycle vandal. The next time, a
cowboy, red bandana flaming around his neck.

A village simpleton tosses a few sous
to the little girl who'll go with him
into the ditch

a game called *lait caillé*
curdled milk

Someone snitches and the law steps in and here's where Foucault
goes red in the face

—

Foucault said fuck normalcy and who wouldn't agree? BUT IT'S TOO
SLIPPERY! THERE'S NOTHING TO HOLD ON TO! discipline,
he said, is a form of power that threatens us to behave "normally" or
else: prisons, schools, office buildings, barracks, mental hospitals too—
all built for surveillance, all built to ward them off, those bright raging
flashes of transgression

Someone always gets thrown under the bus and here
it's little girls, the ones you toss a few coins to for caresses
the older ones won't give. *Caresses*
is a sweet word. Language
is everything

Bucolic, harmless, inconsequential.
Délectations buissonières.

Thrown under the bus for the greater theory
the State should keep its fingers out of sexuality—
it is not the business of the law

Foucault shakes his fist as the village simpleton is carried off
to a mental hospital, no better than prison

Skeptical of boundaries he asks, could children's sexuality
really be hermetically sealed off from adults'?

Questioning is seductive. Challenging, transgressing
even more so—pure fire

HOW QUICKLY IT CAN TURN

Edge of arrogance, chisel-edge

NO QUESTION KAMENEFF TOOK WHAT HE COULD
AND HEADED FOR THE OPEN SEAS

He said they were all equals
BUT

yes to pleasure who wouldn't say yes to more
pleasure BUT

BUT—

Afraid of a "society of dangers," a number of intellectuals
presented a petition to the French parliament in 1977
calling for the abolition of the age of consent.
Signed: Foucault, Sartre, de Beauvoir, Robbe-Grillet, etc.

Would Foucault defend Léo?

～

Childhood stolen all its milk caps Coke bottles bottle rockets off the
back of a bike

This thing called childhood, invented, a compartment
we think is hermetically sealed but then
there's always leaking
always transgression

On the Skype screen, seated inside the bulkhead of childhood
constructed in the eighteenth century, reserved for the aristocracy
the boat builder's son peels back the plastic wrapper
around a stick of cheese
inviolate

Words like coaxed cajoled caressed
jam together ugly and suspect
(suddenly a hand)

And then one night
a whole arm pulls you into a bunk
lifts you light as a starfish
scooped from the sea

then two hands
and breath
a voice that's almost recognizable

then a mouth

then under

~

In the daylight no one speaks of it
(you get the rules quick enough)

Silence the surest fetters

≈

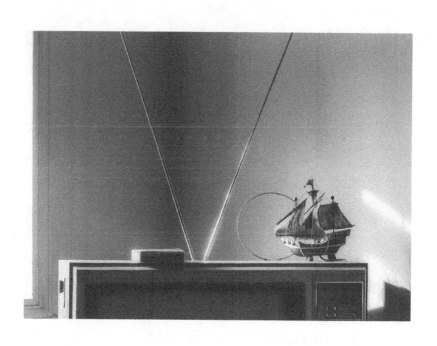

Flotsam & jetsam

This story is built of splinters. Shards
Each one so big

so weighty. Like those super-heavy
elements they make in accelerators

I started piling
tiny toxic layers

mica-thin, sparkling
and deadly

something still tugging me along
something just out of reach—

—

story like an ocean like my rich inward dark

story in my teeth
in my ligaments & bones
in everything that binds us

story the bowl, the undersea filaments, the wind

SUN'S GOING DOWN you trying to get me stirred up JUST REMARKING ON THE FACTS, THE STATE OF THINGS, THE GREATER THINGS, YOU KNOW—WHAT DID 'THE STATE' SAY ABOUT CHILDHOOD what do you mean WHAT WAS IT THAT FOUCAULT OBJECTED TO I have to do some more reading, but in the barest basics, he asked us to step outside the constructs that become invisible, to ask who is behind things YOU MEAN HE JUST WANTED AWARENESS, A WRY EYE right, like a grandfather keeping watch over the trucks that stopped to toss out garbage by the creek WELL THAT SURE SMACKS OF LIVED EXPERIENCE

my grandfather kept a rifle behind the drapes, in the house at the end of the dead-end street (not that it helped, when she needed it. But I don't want to bring my mother into it) WONDER IF YOUR GRANDFATHER WAS A LIBERTARIAN hey—what's the difference anyway between a libertarian and a libertine? don't both of them just want to be free? AND THEY HAVE THE PROVERBIAL GUNS TO DEFEND IT right LIBERTARIANS DEFEND THEIR RIGHT TO TOTAL FREEDOM—SOCIAL, ECONOMIC, FREEDOM OF SPEECH, FREEDOM TO DO ANYTHING—*SO LONG AS IT DOESN'T INFRINGE ON ANYONE ELSE'S* SAID RIGHT and libertines? LIBERTINES ARE INTERESTED IN PHYSICAL PLEASURES. AND THEY DON'T GIVE A FUCK

~

I do believe in childhood I do
believe in the sacred hermetic
precious sealed inside revered

I do want my bulkhead

black, & white

—

But I learned about grey early on
and I learned it in the dead-end street
The street where my grandparents lived

My cousins and I combed the thin
stretch of woods beside the golf course
found garter snakes, golf balls, bottles, shreds
of dirty magazines. We all yelped
at those, all wanted to see more, but couldn't
be seen to want it

I was the brave one with the snake in my hands
cool, lithe, writhing, and I moved
my hands over & over, an infinity

—

I dreamed the moon was surging
toward the Earth

In 2013 they condemned Kameneff to twelve years SO IS HE STILL IN
JAIL? I don't know, I've been trying to find out

—

Dear A.,

The dreams of the moon pressing closer are more and more frequent,
themselves pressing in, and one night walking up the steep arc of Parc
Ave. it hit me—if the moon (white circle perfect over the mountain)
were closer, everyone would be trying to own it.

—

Waiting to speak to the boat builder
The story waiting

—

The day I almost drowned
I was stuck in the break

no *repères* anywhere, no up or down, self
or sea, just water and gasping
air

hauling with all my strength
but all my strength was nothing
against the ocean

SIRENS WOKE ME THIS MORNING—THE DANGER KIND, NOT THE MERMAID KIND, THOUGH I GUESS IT'S FAIR TO CALL THEM BOTH DANGEROUS do you think sirens were named after the Sirens? I'LL ASK WHEN I DROP *MOBY'S DICK* OFF AT THE LIBRARY taking a break from the toxic sea? THE WEB *IS ACTUALLY* IN THE SEA YOU KNOW—THERE'S NO CLOUD, JUST MILES AND MILES OF CABLES, THE MAJORITY OF THEM ON THE MYSTERY OF THE OCEAN FLOOR

YES, TAKING A BREAK. THOUGH I DID POP ON THE OLD NET SURFBOARD FOR JUST A MOMENT YESTERDAY AND HOLY CANNOLI GET THIS what THEY'RE MAKING *SHOES* OUT OF THE PLASTIC ISLANDS NOW

—

H. comes to visit at the white tower
I make cocktails—sour cherries soaked in vodka
We add sprigs of fresh cilantro at the last
raise glasses to all our various forms of heartbreak

human and non-human. H. was the first to tell me
about the plastic islands. "We have to reimagine
our relationship to plastic, because it's going to be around
for a long time."

She's made a career of studying it
travels for conferences all over the world

Underwater synth sound of Skype ringing
and then there he is, in the coach house

behind the house, with his walls of records
multiple guitars and amps, the boy musician's dream

There was a song we used to sing together on the mossy porch
once at the bar full o' boat builders. Or rather

he played and I sang, only I could never remember the second verse
and now I think it might have been because he was missing the chord

that would have carried me in
There ain't nothing can harm you

He'd be wearing his tweed cap, fingers flying across the solo
I'd be looking out past the blackberry vines at the moon

—

Song can cause you to think of so many times and melodies and mouths,
and maybe it is no mystery that we feel so bare singing, like we're giving
the truest of ourselves away, like a bird is flying out of our chests and
gone

—

I am on my own, everyone is an island

When you start talking about transgression suddenly it will never stop, one in four, there's just so much. It silences, it really does, and no wonder tears come to my mother's eyes to think about singing beautifully, something she believes she's never done

~

I don't really want to bring my mother into it, I'm just telling the truth for the moment

~

I don't want to bring my mother into it

~

Some people cling fiercely to song like it could save them. The whales' song could save them if they weren't cut off. Why don't I want to say it out loud. It's because of what people might think. Same as when I sang onstage at the bar full o' boat builders and felt that bird leaving me what will they think what will they think? I can never get it back once it's gone

It's in the coach house that he has the old magazine from the boat
the one with the photo of him and the whale. He pulls it out

after a moment's search, and holds it up to the computer's camera:
his fifteen-year-old self floating beside the whale—

which in truth was not a mother
but a humpback calf.

⁓

There he is: a creature among creatures, gangly, connected
It's in these moments I start to feel

I'm teetering on a narrow path
with loose stones

These stories are real and not just my own

⁓

Eight years later I say
I never stopped thinking about you
swimming to see the eye

"Yeah, the eye. And all
the barnacles, the scars, from rocks and hulls.

"A floating microcosm," he says,
"a whole planet unto itself."

I tried to push this story away

I wanted the whale, the eye
and I wanted to leave it

whole

—

I gave myself three days—no more—to follow the sharp
turn. Three days for the story to show me that it needed to be
    followed.

And if at the end I still felt the resistance, I would leave it.
But see—here we are now—

≈

Story: Oooooo… oooooo

I: Yes, I get it. You're haunting me.

Story: Oooooo! And I have nothing of the womb-cave.

I: You're hard to pin down. I'm digging and digging and trying to get to the bottom.

Story: Don't forget: I am a puzzle that must be left unsolved.

I: You might want to think about a second career. Involving purple robes and crystal balls.

Story: More like crystal bowls. The task is to strike them and let them ring. A question—what's in this, really, for you?

The beginning—no, further back

Go back to the beginning

is there a further back than this?

that other island, a tent
my mother and my father—

is there something further? is there a thin
skin of water flowing endlessly?

Me, a pearl in the inland sea.
All was dark and sure.

Sometimes night is the surest thing there is.

～

Whose truths are these?
Shake yourself out like a shoe.
Not all of this belongs to you.

～

Heart beating
when the body is the size of a grain of rice.
Chambered, already.

How do you shield someone who's inside you
from what's inside you?

Despair I don't know how to shake,
tipped over like an old shoe.

⁓

Elements added, osmosed—outside, the plantain
grows day by day, matching the child
millimetre for millimetre.

The wild rhubarb. Forsythia blooming at her birth.

—added, osmosed, the elbows
can bend now, and the knees. The name has changed.
Embryo to fetus

(how do you shield?)

Write a word on the walls of this room
your body is making, first house for the pearl-fetus,
choose a good word, a strong word, a word that comes in a good way

(how do you shield someone?)

Loon calls. Stars call. Heed the stars' call on this island, swim.
What you can't see can hurt you

but it won't, not tonight. No rapture
like the rapture of night silk water
and your body, suspended between stars.
How lucky we will have been

O grant her the gift of witnessing as we have witnessed
lakes of deepest black, one far-off wave and all is dark—
for that is what the future is, and the best thing it can be—
except the wave is light, and inside the wave
their leaping dark-finned joy,
and just this once, a baby.

O grant her the gift of phosphorescence
of innocence again.

—

Rapture and joy. Can't you see I'm desperate.

Inside the wave the heart beats, chambered already.

The heart howls, restless as a wolf to escape.
Waits with the sleeping patience of a wolf
ears cocked. Ready at any moment to leap.

Knees and elbows bend, the space between stars
stays constant.

No it doesn't. Nothing alive stays constant.

—

Did I choose the whale, or did the whale choose me?

≈

In his own words

Enfants, je ne crois pas à votre minorité.

So writes Kameneff in his manifesto, *Écoliers sans tablier*.
Children were not lesser, were not minor, were just the same as adults.

A teacher, who became a child psychologist,
he had a vision.

J'ai imaginé un séjour de rupture à bord d'un bateau—
an alternative to traditional school, rich in discovery

for those who dare to take the risk.
The site for the *École* is still online. It's full of promises:

Une experience émancipatrice. Vivre ensemble sans hiérarchie.
Erasure of the boundaries. Freedom from hierarchy.

At first it was just for troubled youth
and then for anyone aged nine to sixteen,

all of them looking for adventure.

⁓

The *École en bateau* was born, he said, of the ideals of '68,
windswept sunsmashed radical free.

Many of the victims hint at
the inexpressible

beauty
of the thing.

A life they lived, a journey they can't
explain

or erase.
They came back changed.

⁓

La société a vraiment changé.
Des choses qui paraissaient normales à l'époque, éducatives, sont regardées
aujourd'hui avec suspicion, comme être nus à bord.

Being naked on board and all the things that made the boat builder falter.
"It wasn't hidden," says Kameneff during the trial, "and it wasn't sexual."
C'était du naturisme familial, sans connotation sexuelle, la recherche d'une
vie tranquille, paisible.

But then:

Je ne vois aucune raison objective à l'interdiction des rapports sexuels aux enfants. On violente pas mal au nom de l'éducation. Le sexe, ce serait quand même plus caressant.

THIS ONE BEARS TRANSLATING DIRECTLY hm... although I know, as a translator myself, that "translating directly" is all but impossible—you're right:

I see no objective reason to forbid sexual relations with children. There's so much violence committed in the name of education. Sex, at least, would be more affectionate.

In court, he plays with words

REMIND YOU OF ANYONE?

The accused denies any pedophilic act, saying
The pedophile doesn't care at all about the child—the child has no import-ance to him.

Defence: *And if not pedophilic attraction, then what can you call it?*

The accused: *Play, affection.*

THE TREACHERY OF WORDS

The accused: *Yes, some of my actions were objectionable, but it was never pedophilic attraction.*

About the massages, he explains that *caresses sometimes cause an erection, we fondle each other a little and we laugh about it.*

These words keep ringing:
affection, jeu, sensualité.

Defence: *Are you sexually attracted to children?*

The accused: *I think I would be lying if I gave a straightforward answer to this question. Between parents and children, there can be a kind of attraction—it's a difficult boundary to establish.*

If we feel tenderness and affection toward others, it's possible for that to go a little further...

For the first three days of trial
he sidestepped, pussyfooted

Then on the fourth day the boy with eyes still broken
took the stand. The boy he'd favoured. Boy-
become-man, always a trembling
at the corners, eyes slipping

to the sides, he stuttered out the ways
his own life has been fettered

Finally K.
cracked

Hand to his head he said
sorry

Words, sometimes all-powerful
other times empty balloons

They give nothing back

≈

Le Petit Voyageur

**Réalisé par le groupe Jules Verne
et l'Ecole en Bateau**

*TRAVERSEE DE L'ATLANTIQUE:
les secrets de Colomb*

N° 82 Octobre 1989 35 FF

ISSN 0290 - 3350

The language of transgression

For them, lexicon of compass
lexicon of nutmeg and limes

For the boat builder, lexicon of language, French words
separate from his body

Words that kept him apart
Like peering in a window

A little bit secret
a little bit glass

The far-off hammer
le marteau au loin à travers la baie

—

I studied translation beside
Cézanne's mountain

culled (from *cueillir,* to gather) rosemary, *sauge*
thyme, *marjolaine.* Shaped

my mouth around consonnes et voyelles
taught my ears the difference between

[ø] and [œ], *c'est pas la mer*
à boire

I drank a thousand
café crèmes and smoked a thousand

gauloises jaunes & still I never fully
learned the codes

—

Between languages, Brault says, *il y a l'espace de la*
créativité, space of sparking. *Je le vois sombre*
in the way darkness streams
with everything we find magic:

secret trout,
a spirit that knows something about us

—

Steeped in language, holding up my dress,
je flirte avec cette autre, but what lies
between them and where

do the stunned blind wordless gashes go
when someone comes in the night
saying *if it feels good…*

That's not the pure potential, no
That's not the mystic space between, no

That clangs and locks and shudders
and goes blank

or blinding, sun on shining
flanks *je m'imaginais nager avec les baleines.*

It is possible to leave your body

~

The reefs swallow, sway, forests
on the sea floor

compass set to deeper currents
you could drift

far out of sight
yellow violet stripes

flash of fish
before it hides

branches of coral
reaching like hair

silence of the green swaying
miles and miles

peer down into valleys
water becomes sky

stillness (stay still)
hundreds of tiny white fish like snow

worlds and worlds down there,
cathedrals full of rooms (inviolate)

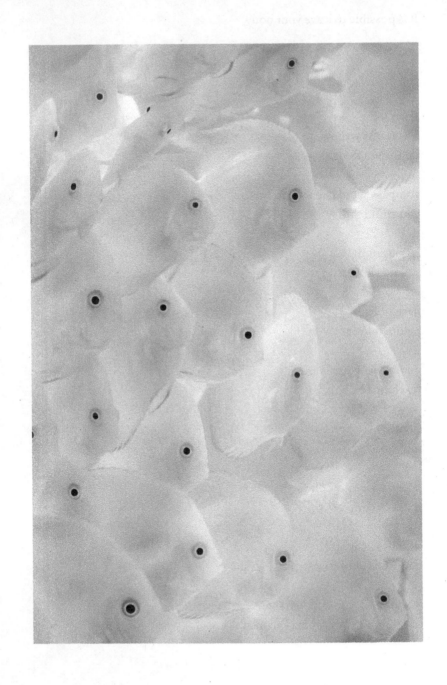

We: Have you been here long?

Transgression: Since before you were born.

We: Would they condemn you before?

Transgression: Not in every age, nor through every door.

We: What do you get from it?

Transgression: A feather. A journey. A crossing of space. There are tastes you wouldn't know if you hadn't let me in.

We: What do you want?

Transgression: To crackle the ribs. The foundations. To cross borders. I don't care if I'm believed. How did you come to know all you say you know, if what you say is true?

We: Staying still as stones while you went barging through all the borders, we saw.

Transgression: If everyone stayed inside their skins, inside their countries, their riverbanks, their shores—

We: Yes? Yes?

Transgression: —they'd learn only the inward walls. Nothing—no air balloons, no circus tents, no telephones, no feats of light— would ever come.

We: ...

Transgression: No Friday nights, no transvestites, no holy rolling preacher men, no disco balls, no derby dolls, no knowing of the Earth as round, no stalactites, no sodomites, no kinship with the moon and sun, no dinosaurs, retracting floors, no change, no new ideas at all.

We: Is this some kind of trick?

—

Foucault strides into the classroom motorcycle jacket leather pants cigarette dangling FOUCAULT LOVED MEN WHEN LOVING MEN WOULD NOT JUST GET YOUR TEETH KICKED IN wish we could say that time was past SO YEAH, HE KNEW TRANS-GRESSION

He just wanted to break everything apart

≈

Groundswell

THERE'S MORE, THOUGH I know, I was trying to keep things hermetic—there's something from childhood something just out of reach something about not wanting to hold everything not all the eggs in one basket THOSE EGG-SHAPED STONES YOU USED TO COLLECT maybe it's when my mother told me—I already carried a great deal, keeping things separate, ordering the world JUST TELL IT HOW YOU LIVED IT. START FROM THE START

—

There were the secret underwater passages where I was—happy—
if you can call a fissure in rock *happy*
a thing without edges

the silence down there—no, the sound
a hum like those huge hovering
bumblebees (far-off boats)

click like the lift of the needle
from the record (when I picked the stem
of a lily or lake grass)

like there would never be an end
and I plucked them stem by stem
myself hovering, royal, in secret green light

There was, too, my pact with the dark
An innate understanding. (My right eye
cries for ever having lost it)

How I descended fearless into the old basement
how I became the still point
and how many times I dreamed that pitch-dark passage

dark as the way into a dream itself
or that time sleeping at my grandfather's house
when I woke before anyone else

and the darkness made itself known to me
placeless and spreading
familiar and warm

I came down the staircase like stepping into water—
it spread out fully as water does, with another kind of hum—
the dark rose to meet me

⁓

Day is nasturtiums

(orange yellow falling
all over itself)

dark has this heart and tender
sound

(if you close your eyes
if you lean in close)

I descended to meet it
slip of a shadow within shadow

unseen

I listen back to the recording of my last conversation with the boat builder. I can't believe I forgot what he said about Kameneff. That he was out already in 2016, three years after the trial, for reasons unpublished, probably to do with his health, *l'ancienneté des faits*. *That was short!* I hear myself exclaim.

I hear his excitement at the project. At the ready with pen and paper, making a list of what to send me. Pages from the logbook. Photographs. Postcards.

And maybe the recorded conversation was most revealing not of him, but of me. It's revealing how little I *do* reveal. And when I do talk about the book, the book becoming, how cautious I am with my words. Chosen carefully to show I hold his story like a child with a hot bowl of soup in two hands.

≈

The shores of the world

The shores of the world are different now

not like when I was young

my palette was pale stone
beach glass seaweed not

hot pink aqua atomic orange—
more plastic than fish in thirty years, they say—

~

The waters compassed me about

~

The whale dreams began when I was still a child

    always from shore always racing to see them

leaping dark joy in waves
hurled through with light

"Sperm whales found full of car parts and plastics"
"Adidas 3-D printed shoe from ocean waste"
"Drowning in plastic"

Then I ask the question
eyes what do you want
and when they answer
I turn away

H. says they are discovering new organisms
with adaptable digestive systems
and all at once it blasts into me foolish and reckless

hope

—

I am a needle   I am a pivoting sensing needle floating

I skip past videos of the arctic ice melting

—

The waters compassed me about, even to the soul

—

One of Kameneff's victims said this: *dans ma tête je hurlais* non
je m'imaginais nager avec les baleines

A whale song can go on
for over an earthly year
can you even think of it?

—

Hydrophones under arctic ice trace long underwater lines of song

Mournful circus whistles
blades of grass
juicerators
trapped birds
scream-sighs mouth closed silver-
white wails gurgles
hauntings

—

THEY'VE BEEN DOCUMENTING THE HAVOC WREAKED
ON WHALES BY LOUD SOUNDS—A SINGLE MILITARY
HIGH-FREQUENCY TEST CAN CAUSE A WHALE TO
BECOME PERMANENTLY DISORIENTED

Sending out sonar
swift across kilometres, Azores to Newfoundland
Newfoundland to the Beaufort Sea, swift and ricochet
wave and inlet, cave and cave and plummet
there are creatures we have never seen

A whale does not know itself by seeing
but by sound

Music drowns

⁓

THEY'RE WASHING UP IN TOFINO, EARDRUMS BURST

⁓

The waters compassed me about, even to the soul
the depths closed me round about

H. talks about the split—

put your head in a cloud and feel it
stuff your ears full of water and microbeads

—the split, where all that you're studying, absorbing
is disaster

and meanwhile this life
this luxury pleasant nice house nice bed good food travel all
over the aching world

~

DID YOU KNOW THAT WHALES HAVE AN EXTREMELY
HIGHLY DEVELOPED CEREBRAL CORTEX—THE PART
OF THE BRAIN RELATED TO MEMORY, EMPATHY AND
CONSCIOUS THOUGHT?

~

I am a storm   caught by the storm   in a swivelling so strong
it reaches spirit

what happens when the sea is full of other sounds? THEIR RADIUS OF COMMUNICATION SHRINKS—ACOUSTIC SMOG, AS THEY CALL IT, CAN REDUCE A WHALE'S RANGE FROM 2,600 KILOMETRES TO 400 what if one is lost? THAT'S JUST IT LOST

—

Je m'imaginais nager avec les baleines

—

The day I saw it, I was chasing the sunset again
reeling with all the boat builder had told me
those eight years later, headed onward

up the Oregon coast.
Knuckles of rocks pushed through
sand, silky miles—

I smelled it first. Gulls swirl
down, hop and peck.
I photographed the dead

whale, orange and grey, half
gone. The massive fact
of death. Gulls screaming, pecking

sun landing on the rot.
I had been waxing
to the ocean's wild yes

not thinking of rising acidity
industrial waste
or plastic cups.

Then there it was: the orange stinking mass
with one of two messages: this is a killing ocean
or, there is rot in every perfect thing.

I went on, over cold sand, leaving my boots
behind a rock, I went on pretending
I was having a rapturous time.

I set the camera into clefts of stone
and feigned being breathless and overjoyed.

⁓

The waters compassed me about, even to the soul
the depths closed me round about, the weeds were wrapped about my head

⁓

When I came close to the scorched
rotting mass all pecked
all flurried round with birds

I looked
for the eye—

found the ragged
leaking hole

I am not only that which I see but I hold all of it

The whole and the broken, the singing and the rotting
I am all of it. Praises be sung
to the abyss, the deepest
trench, the dung heap of our nature
the night terrors—

nothing so horrifying as something different
in the shape of someone you know

≈

I have a room in the dark

I was born to this

I was in my narrow bed when she told me
My room with fake wood panelling big black
carpenter ants that sometimes crawled out
like she believed I was destined for the same fate
and by God she would stop it this time
What words did she use?

All I know is she wanted to keep me safe
All I know is she wanted me to save her

In the awful world I watched for it
watched from the age of eight, seven, six
When I was six a boy pinned me down until
I kissed him. Winded on my narrow bed

I used all my strength
but all my strength was nothing

That song with the sax was on the radio
and for years and years I couldn't hear it without
my stomach turning

I saw a grey wolf once
when I was alone
At the edge of a field thick with goldenrod
and purple loosestrife

I was a child allowed to walk alone then
We will seek out whatever thickets we can, we'll run to them
The strip between Jane Street and the golf course was mine

Just as it was my mother's
and all her sisters' and brothers'
at the end of the dead-end street, thirty years before

Patterns pull us
patterns form us—

History lies
very close—so close you can't
look it in the eye

How does any predator become?

Quiet in the rushes
waist-high and cutting
quiet in the stars
of purple loosestrife—

is hunger always dark?

I have a room in the dark it's there like a worm
like a beginning way, way down
as a child she was at the neighbour's
inside that room

No one chooses their hunger
they choose their compass

when you're dead no one can prove
what side you're on

when you're a thousand miles from shore no one can save you
when you're in the next house over no
no one

~

I remembered a yellow blanket yesterday. Soft well-washed cotton, spread tight over patterned sheets. My mother liked making the bed. Thin stripe of light blue at the border of my yellow blanket. Cotton-clean smell. Pale as spring against the dark wood panelling. When that ant came out it bit into my arm and would not let go. I screamed and she came in a red rush and pulled it off me. It took a piece with it. That's what I remember. I remember a hole in my arm where the ant bit.

I was young when she told me
I don't even know how old
I tiptoed around it
I'm tiptoeing around it now

the terrible faraway fact and every now and then I wanted
details

Even if it felt light years
away, even if I believed unswervingly
in her

still
I could feel—

she was a branch and the words out loud were an ice storm

I could harm her again
if I said the wrong thing

⁓

REMEMBER HOW IT WAS WHEN YOU WERE A KID? THE
WILD FREEDOM. THE WAY YOU COULD RIDE FASTER
THAN THE FASTEST SPEEDBOAT ON THE BACK OF YOUR
BEST FRIEND'S SLED AND NEVER BE AFRAID OF SLAMMING
INTO A ROCK—REMEMBER? but also the richness of fear, the way
terror could squeeze the logic clean out of you—when it came, fear was
a blue whale, bigger than anything, and then there was your mother's
voice, her hand turning on the bedside lamp, and only she could save
you—and only if she stayed

Darkness has
a presence I said
day is just

the absence of
presence why
is that?

Day is nasturtiums
night is
terrifying

⁓

I didn't used
to be afraid

of the dark
no I descended
to meet it

⁓

And in the day the garden
sun and o the shade

Borage & mugwort, lamb's
quarters, mullein

so much sustenance
so many healers

The way a worm feels unearthed
the way a shard of glass feels
caked with dirt

—

Sometimes night is a trap: you are waiting and waiting for day to
release you (Proust knew it) and it never comes

it's like night is the basket for all our fears. all it carries FEAR THAT
BLACK FLAPPING HEART-PUMPING IRON FIST

night   a basket   alive   put your wriggling thumping

fears in here   wait   for day

—

She was still so young
and she sprouted the seeds
and she made her own bread
and she made her own yogurt
and by God she was going to change the pattern this time

All I know is she wanted to keep me safe

She, a pretty shape in my dark room
light from the kitchen leaning in

~

child
only
child

~

Let, I beg you
let your child be sometimes invisible

~

Oh—my mother too—always seeking rapture
All my life her exclamations about the moon

The cold white moon. Sometimes that is her

Then I have no key
none at all

My inmost never-ending

measure

mother

～

When they were kids
they shared a bedroom
my mother and her two sisters

only one stayed asleep

the other sat straight up in the dark and rattled
drawers or walked down the hall turning
doorknobs or just stood

still eyes open unseeing

beside the bed where my mother lay cold awake.
She talked sometimes but you weren't
supposed to talk back

nothing so horrifying as something different
in the shape of someone you know—

And me—many nights I lay awake and terrified
waiting

—

Ford and forge ahead beneath thickets through
stars of loosestrife I saw
a wolf once when I was ten
out walking alone

Neither of us hungered

—

Drawers rattling, footsteps
praying at dawn,
dawn like fruit broken open
juice streaming
down. Kingbirds

wake me and I ride to the lake's edge to see it, sunrise
over the shores of the world,
sand and trash and seaweed
in the morning light all
tangled

The waves cough up
another bag, the sandpipers
peck and peck

All in one lifetime!

It is possible to acclimatize too easily
who wants to hold horror
in the mouth too long

⁓

We sail on
light as paper
nighttime ocean

Ocean without fish
without stars
without plastic

Ocean of ignorance
Close your eyes

There was a time when a palm reader warned me
some of what I carry is not my own

He said I was the falcon
but hooded

Three guesses who the falconer was

—

One of these days I'll have to

let her off
the
hook

Turning and turning in the widening gyre
now the size of middle Europe, they say

they say "The Great Pacific Garbage Patch"
as though there's something to celebrate.

Five ocean gyres and all of them
trash—

～

At a certain point, they say, your work
your healing
is done for someone
else

～

I remember the clay loam of the path along the fence after I saw the
wolf—the packed-earth smell, the mud that gripped my sneaker
treads—I didn't know the words *clay loam* then, but I remember
looking down at the ropes of green vine gone dusty brown and stuck in
the edges of the path and everything was so thick and I was so alive to it

Such heat the day I saw the wolf, such sound

There at the end of the dead-end street
with the house next door I had my wilderness.
Beside the stairs up to Jane Street.

I didn't mind the garter snakes, yellow
stripe down their backs, pure sinew
smooth through my hands. I was brave then.

My cousins and I did flips over the handrails,
just a thin strip of forest between the stairs and the golf course
but it was ours. Our parents', too. The road they grew up on.

You could say she grew up fast.
You could say she was a child no more.

But this is also true: she was caught
(in the dark room dark as a worm as a beginning)
small and silent, trapped there forever.

(and always my mother and a quarter of my mind will be a girl inside
that room)

All my life I've carried the dark
room. Darker

shape. Hand
mouth

her, tiny, all
my life this skittering sickening room

Not mine

In the morning she walked back
across the lawn

my grandfather never knew
no, he never knew

the gun hung useless
behind the drapes

silence the surest fetters
you get the rules quick enough

We know the shallows
caught fish that turn in the heat

we know what's spent
to arrive at the still point

fifty years after he robbed it from us:
the goldfinch that sings a whole

shoreline. Childhood. We know the key
that never fits any lock

we know drawers rattling
footsteps praying at dawn

They say we have cathedrals inside
with infinite rooms

I like this version better

Sometimes it seems we all have
skin stretched to the limit

flesh that's turned
a thousand crawling transgressions

Rot in every perfect thing

≈

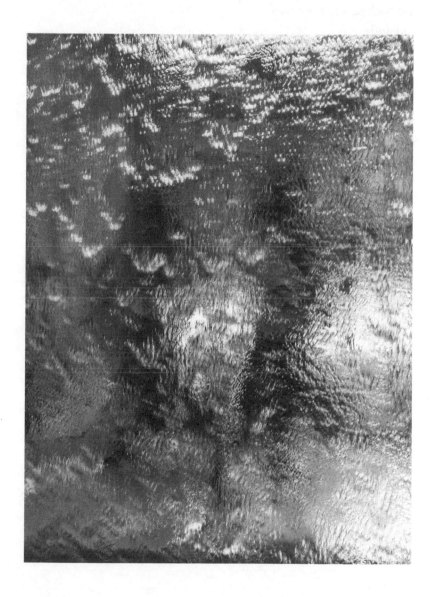

Other voices

Go back now to the ocean
quietude

enter and there's no
divide

How the boat builder would dive in
liquid like darkness

compassing him about until
he, too, had no edges

Sensing the whales, even when they
were out of sight

—

THE LONG SONGS OF FIN AND BLUE WHALES OFTEN
HAVE A RHYMING STRUCTURE. MAKES YOU WONDER
WHETHER THAT'S A METHOD FOR REMEMBERING, MUCH
AS IT IS FOR HUMANS

Sometimes we sing
and nothing—

not laughing, not crying, not loving—
makes us feel closer

when I sing that ribbon reaches out
my sound waves move your body's cells

bridge of sound, erasing distance

sounds begin before we're born
sounds inside the inland sea

I have sung the same songs for years, songs
like smooth caves

like unchanging caves if we want them to be

~

Last night at the gallery
H. and I heard humpbacks sing—

pulses and pings and clicks of rhythm
long arcing notes o, the sea would be full.
Tall tousle-haired boy at his soundboard remixing

that famous ecologist's field recordings. Afterwards, soft night
rolled cigarettes, offhand finery, I tell him about the eye
and he reminds us it's all about hearing.

Of course. A whale does not know itself through seeing
but through sound. "If I were to echolocate you now,"
he says, holding my eye, pulling on his thin cigarette,

"it would be an image of your face that was produced
through sound waves." If I were to echolocate you.
A deep V flushes through me.

He tells me of a magic machine that reproduces images
from sound through water. A machine that can make
an image of what a whale sees from the sound it emits.

He says scientists are planning to send whales
the sound images of trees. Cross-realm visuals. H. hoots,
then winces. What would an aqueous brain make of these?

Something surges in me midway through the songs.
Soaring chest-full notes in the minor. The vastness,
rapturous and piercing at once

making music out of the voices of these mammals
in a chic gallery in Montreal
two plastic water bottles on the table beside him

≈

The key that never fits any lock

I'm not actually sure when she told me
I said *eight seven six* because it was somewhere around there, and now
it's too brittle, too bleeding, to ask

The question will come as a blade

All she wanted was to keep me safe

~

Rooftops aching and arrows

I must say I'm advancing in the great *tâtonnement*, tap-tap-tapping
no map, no knowing, just a subliminal urge
and the eaves tap-tapping, and the far-off thunder
and the curtain of rain

I must admit I don't know where I'm going

Most tender devastating

mirror

mother

〜

There's something I…

〜

I showed her a section, to get her yea or nay
before I showed anyone else—
"That's all I want for right now," I said
"I can't really talk about it yet"

See, I have become protective of the fleshy white
story, of what it wants to be. I can't follow the stream through the fen
if I'm standing guard for someone else

But God. It plagues and trails
behind me, a broken snail

Whose stories do we have the right to tell?

～

Yea, came her reply
And later we speak again

She forms words
I think of a tiny inchworm
at the tip of a finger

I think you got it wro... she stops herself
I think you misunderstood
I didn't need you to save me

There was a theory circulating, when I was young
that the child may relive the parent's trauma when she reaches the age
the parent was

I told you so you would have some understanding
if you were feeling the same things

We are on the phone. My jaw nearly drops
Because if I remember, I think she was five when it happened

～

I can't ask her now. It would be like pulling out a sword.

How do you protect someone who made you?

~

My mother, who all my life would draw in
a rushing breath, making me startle, saying,
Look! The moon, look at the moon!

My mother who tended the comfrey-
furred green giant at the back of the yard
who taught me how to use it
plantain too—crush the leaves for a cut or sting

My mother who held tightly to beauty
who crouched beside me, both our hands in the dirt
the roots and rocks and exquisite worms
preparing the ground for something new

~

I began to watch differently
The world was full of slithering intentions
I didn't have to look far

~

This story is hers, but it is also my own

I dream of them again
All is dark, all is so dark, like the future
is dark, and the boat beneath my feet
is taking on water

Only in the far-off is there light—
a wave shot through with green-gold light
and they are there, their leaping dark joy

And this time, tumbling with them
a child

—

I walked past a house yesterday
where they were digging up the whole front yard
and the smell—wet, dark, clean, brown, deep
—took me to another time

A time of white flowers pouring over the fence
spirea's round petals rain smell of chalk and spring &
burdock's booming robust stalks & shepherd's purse
eat its tiny green hearts. Medicine

The two of us, content in the garden

Sun burning away the nighttime threat of the bad
things people could do to you

This is an old story—a child, a secret weight
the way it sheds
into everything

This is an old story—the whale, awe
beneath the surface, the way we lean toward
something greater

⁓

I think I've always been searching to one day be so busted up with
rapture

I'd be saved

⁓

Can the story ever be greater than the teller?

And we—
do we ever become more than the stories we contain?

We know the beasts half-hidden
and we know the golden beach

we know what's half-buried
taunting, out of reach

We know the curl of wave that bends the light
we know the cough of wave

We know what was lost
cannot be unlost

We know what you are avoiding even as
your eyes scurry off

we know Foucault would have scoffed
but it's true all the same

—

I asked her one time
for his name.

Silence on the line.

Why? she finally says. *He has kids. Grandkids.*
I don't want to give you his last name.

She and her siblings called him Uncle Ben.

There's something I...

There's something I forgot...

There's something I forgot to say...

≈

Un séjour de rupture

In my white tower, on a grey day, I watch the documentary again
Enter the Vimeo password, see their open faces. Within the adult
the child, looking out.

Every moment of rapture now suspect.

More than one has thought of suicide.
They all remember
the rule of the king.

Now this unending desire
to please. Can't shake it off or
set it down.

One leafs through his logbook, *carnet de bord*, beginning
with thrill and light and inching toward
a page filled with insults

hurled at the other kids. And then. The day
he was first down below with Léo:
a blank page.

Never an entry again.

The defenceless smiling eyes of the one in a hat.
How he hid behind the kitchen door the day he got home.
His mother went looking all through the house.

In the end he went back. It was all he could do.
Back to the boat and the people who knew, the ones among whom
it made sense.

Logic is a trap.
Heartlessly evident

in the writings of most philosophers, logic is both
the pleasure of the thing and the reason to hate them.

Foucault plays with the trap and keeps it open
refusing to be one thing. One theory. One identity.

Always slipping away.

—

*How can it be that over all these years not a single parent
came raging?* one man asks. *How can it be that they closed
their eyes, pulled all the punches?*

The *École*: straight out of '68, that oasis
that libertine vision of freedom.
Who gets to have it?

The ship in its slight fade glides across the screen
a boy clambers to the top of the mast
his shadow slides behind the sail, moves in shadow

I thought I was free

A smaller boat pulls away, holding only one child
one man. Out in the open there is only grey
No sound in this shot but I hear:

If you say anything it will hurt me a great deal
It will hurt all of us

⁓

The boat builder delivers a message for me
to the author of the book.

He was on board for five years. Beginning at age nine.
I ask about the joy and the nightmare.

He replies: *J'ai vécu quinze ans avec juste les choses extraordinaires. Les*
horreurs, je les connaissais, mais je les balayais sous le tapis, elles n'avaient
pas voix au chapitre.

Fifteen years of exaltation. Of bottling. And then—

Ensuite, j'ai ouvert la boite de Pandore, à la suite de quoi j'ai vécu dix ans
avec juste les horreurs. Elles occultaient tout le reste, il n'y avait plus qu'elles.

Ten years of horror eclipsing all the rest.

How do we hold both?

In the documentary, the author of the book says he lost
innocence—no *repères* inside or out

The first time he changed his own child's diaper his hands shook

The door had to be open always

> open and the kids

could never sit
on his lap

> He didn't trust himself

to be alone with his own children

—

How do you shield someone made of you
from what's inside you?

—

His nightmares stopped after the trial

> and haven't returned

We are the product of everything that has come before
we hold it all—

in what way, then, does freedom ever exist?

The boat builder's son squawks somewhere off-screen
my friend's face up close, distracted
by the next generation

~

He sifts through the boxes his wife knew nothing about

- Watercolour illustration of a sea serpent
- Hand-drawn map
- Postcards with scrawled greetings from boys, from Bernard,
  from Léo: *Joyeuse année!*

~

The boat builder left in '91—the last correspondence
from the *Karrek Ven* was in 2000

Then an empty space

"I know it's not like there was one thing," he says, hands
holding a round invisible, "and that I was outside of it."

"I know the kids from the boat did not stay tight.
It separated us, all of us, there was no…"

no what?

⁓

I ask him to tell me the names of each of the boys in the photo
he just sent. Of one of them,
standing naked and blond at the tip of the prow,

he says only, "He is generally considered to be not a good guy."
"Why not a good guy?" I prod, and he says, "Well,
he kind of became one of the abusers."

Lines go blurry

No one told him about the trial, he had to find out
by chance.

When he left the boat he was
forgotten
written off
shut out

as though it had never been.
My lost year at sea.

Lost. To be a seeker you have to be prepared to…
to be a warrior you have to be prepared to…
to love you have to…

—

"And who's in this one?" I ask.
He names them: Léo, Bernard,
my best friend on board,
the author's little brother.

Two others no one has contact with anymore—
they testified for Léo.

≈

Karrek Ven vous offre son univers !

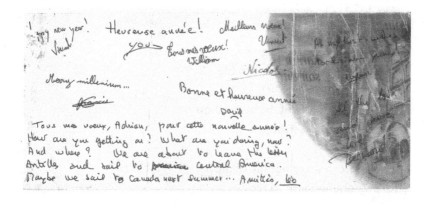

Happy new year! Heureuse année! Meilleurs vœux!
Sisal   Vincent
            you → Tous mes vœux!
                        William
                                        Nicolas
    Merry millenium...
                            Bonne et heureuse année
        Francis
                                    David
    Tous mes vœux, Adrian, pour cette nouvelle année!
    How are you getting on? What are you doing, now?
    And where? We are about to leave the West
    Antilles and sail to Central America.
    Maybe we sail to Canada next summer... Amitiés, Léo

The organ on the porch

On the porch the boys smoked
rattled

Bodies of boats lay here and there in the yard
by the fire pit, cracked seats from an old Dodge

Past the lawn
the wall of blackberries

Dancer the dog with her thick fur heaved in the sun
snapped at wasps

"She gets high on their stings,"
said R. It was his place

He rubbed her belly till she howled
and he howled back

R. would be the next we'd grieve
but that summer he blazed with life

All of them graduates of the boat school
A. built his boat and stayed

neither taciturn sharp nor life of the party
neither rambunctious nor reckless

he had a wide easy smile, loved jazz, and there at the organ
on the porch we had our first conversation, composed

of musical notes. He was earnest. He wasn't embarrassed
to play songs like "Ain't No Sunshine" without irony

That night we all wore silly hats
and ended up at the bar 'til late

three sheets
to the wind

caroused down to Silva Bay
where I learned he was living on his boat

at the end of the wharf
The sea was calm and full of stars

He showed me how to stir the stars
by dropping a penny or pissing

off the edge
the stream flaming green into the dark

Later, inside the hull, he told me the story
I could not have known before

a fearlessness I surged toward
Inside the hull I let that story occupy the space of love

bubbling sounds along the wood
of this boat he'd built with his own hands

We gave each other this
After three nights I woke with the sun

walked to the end of the pier
and boarded a tiny insect of a plane

I was still in love with a dead man
This is what I meant when I said we'd both

been inside a greater love, a greater grief—
still it was comfort

For days after the waves swayed inside my head
inner ears troubled

≈

Neither of us hungered

The wolf is not a threat
not sent to eat you if you tell

The wolf is a key
a stillness
a patch on a quilt I worked on blind

I spent so much time in the dark
in my rich inward dark

I had my doorways, my keys, my secret paths out
through the tunnel of brush on the hill

behind the house my mother grew up in
Steep shadow

No one could touch me

~

The wolf, like the whale
asked nothing

This is what I mean when I say
neither of us hungered

> *They have no feet or hands, nests or lairs, closets or*
> *graves. Fire, stars, and books would never shape*
> *their worlds. What would it mean to live in an*
> *environment immune to shaping and permanence?*
> *What would aqueous mind look and sound like?*
> –John Durham Peters

DID YOU KNOW ABOUT WHALES AND THEIR SEPARATE HEMISPHERES? you mean like migration routes, Arctic and Antarctic? NO I MEAN CONSCIOUSNESS—THE HEMISPHERES OF THEIR BRAINS ARE NOT CONNECTED. MELVILLE BELIEVED, BECAUSE OF THE PLACEMENT OF THEIR EYES, THAT WHALES AND OTHER CETACEANS COULD GET PAST THE LIMITS OF BINARY THINKING

~

Dualism traps enwraps us
either/or, this or that, right or wrong

It is a hard-sprung head-knocking bauble-shaped hard line, binaries
like those wooden figurines rounded on the bottom
when you knock them over they pop back up
and never the twain shall meet

It is solitudes, it is casings, it is black and white
Some things have to be

~

CETACEANS, HE SAID, HAVE EVOLVED TO SEE TWO
SEPARATE REALITIES AT ONCE. DOLPHINS CAN REST A
WHOLE HALF OF THEIR BRAINS BY CLOSING ONE EYE,
AND CAN GO DAYS WITHOUT SLEEPING. PUT THAT IN
YOUR PIPE EH?

AND ON THE SUBJECT OF EVOLUTION—WHALES *RE-TURNED* TO THE OCEAN. EVERYTHING ELSE "EVOLVED"
ONTO LAND.

—

Somehow in twoness they're less divided

humans bounce unendingly
back & forth
this, or that
while in the ocean, creatures swim on

unclipped
unbound

—

Seeming to rise, they fall
seeming to soar, they sink

and only to shore will they keep
pressing and pressing

'til they're dead

it's a trap. binaries are a trap. there can't be just one answer. everything is connected to everything else, we've seen it BUT WE NEED BOUNDARIES OTHERWISE IT'S ALL JUST SLOP. WE NEED BOUNDARIES EVEN THOUGH WE KNOW BLACK AND WHITE IS POPPYCOCK

—

I'm writing this last part under the supermoon
aware, from inside my white tower
of its pull on the tides

here's something that touches
the whales and I

—

I've been carrying this story so long
I don't know how to set it down

If I let it, it would swallow the world and all its blue

I began from a place of needing rapture

badly enough that I'd risk myself under
rooftops and stars and into the hulls of boats

rapture was what tethered me
to the living

when I threatened
to unclip

—

When I was fourteen that palm reader told me
it wasn't up to me to seek it out or make it happen
my destiny would come to me

And that seems to be the way this story rolled up
sea slug tossed ashore and clinging
to the rock. I tried to push it away but it wouldn't let go

I resisted the larger story with teeth
and hands and eyes gone blind—
the first piece, separate, held everything

Whale, daring, exultation—

I haven't explained everything. I've left much unexplained
I wanted to draw your eye
to this:

there is something so much greater than us
and we can choose to swim toward it. I wanted to stop there

I couldn't

—

I am always seeking the way back to a place I've glimpsed only a
handful of times

That feeling of new love there is nothing can compare—
I'd throw myself onto the train tracks

I've thrown myself into the wilderness
over and over and over

I shook a scorpion out of my sleeping bag
I fought a rogue wave and nearly drowned
I flipped a car off the desert highway

I've known grief that shattered me like glass
until I could step into the realm of spirits
I've been broken. Been a crone
when I was still a maiden

Even before that, I knew the need to seek
that rapture-edge
to carry stories as talismans

to stand at the edge of a field
and hold the eye of a wolf

~

You cull and cull weeds on the way to magic
only, your whole life you've known

a weed is just a healer misconstrued
abundance so prolific it's overlooked

The more there is
the less we see. Isn't that funny? The less we love

We thrive off absence like Eros—
deep in our bones we know it's true

You may think you desire the flood
down mountainsides

but it's more likely
the single drop in the desert

the desert where you found the last damned love
cursed and damned eating straight from the can

You may think you want the ocean
but it's the single stone

under your heel that will mark you
show you your contours

All your life you've known
weeds were more valuable than calla lilies

in a gated garden and yes, the first thing you learned
was how to recognize plantain

Crush it, smear it on your skin
we know ourselves by our edges

the lengths to which we're willing to go

And for twenty years I see I've been searching for something
in the arms of men

when I should have been looking over their shoulder
to the places we were in

we bear what we can, and then we
bear it and bear it and bear it, always the same

like a memory of a memory we weather the simulacra
of a sorrow again and again, replicas and replicas and replicas

until—

～

Grief is like that. Grief is your brain flashing
fast between the beloved
and the knowing he is gone, the brutal crack
in the chest. Impossible to know both at once
with our paltry human brains.

And so it is at the heart
of the boat builder's journey, that perfect time
he knows better of, now.

Where is the place where there's room for both
where we can witness them, then lay them down—

What looks like sorrow?
Barnacles. Sorrow is a clinging logic
What does sorrow look like?
The moon, when you chase it in dreams

After I lost the man I loved I dreamed I went to the moon

What was it like there?
Full of emptiness. Full of white waiting. I don't remember
what I wanted to say about sorrow

—

Am I stalled? Am I standing outside the door?

WILL YOU SEIZE THE BRASS HANDLE AND KNOCK ON THE
DOOR OF YOUR OWN LIFE?

There are darknesses at work I can't understand

What I want to know is what it does, hurt,
how it stalls or holds in check—what symptoms
do they see in those who've lost that luminous *before*
and now have this—this always-two so hard to hold
and where and on what shore
can they ever set it down

or do we become receptacles
carrier bags (is this what we are built to be?) the way
storytellers carry tales, and pass them lips to ears—
a glorious ragtag collection—

is it even logical to think our own stories
could be all we hold? or will we always, like chromosomes,
become the well for what has gone before?

⌢

Of course we are built of stories

It's our place in the world
It's a lineage

Shake yourself out like a shoe

⌢

And how, I want to ask, can we hold two truths—
just hold them, side by side, without explaining,
denying, justifying, negating—two truths as though
we had heads with one eye on each side

Talk to a dolphin, I suppose
talk to a whale and see where thinking goes

because (as I have said)
it's possible to swim toward rapture, all at once
it's possible to be regarded, and restored

—

Up close, the oil
of its skin, velvet, captioned black
and dark grey under water, surface scarred
then smooth, alternating
clusters of the
living

a whole planet

—

Water, thank you for teaching me fluidity
a velvet encompassing

Arctic cathedral
roof of ice

one vast chamber
twelve new songs

bowhead whales, back
from the brink of extinction

I see those hydrophones
snaking into the blue

I dive in
no need to breathe

no temperature
& no fear

I take the form I want and my
eye falls on no other human

perhaps here I am not human
perhaps I am more like a skin of water flowing continuously

The whales pass
I look them in the eye, each one

Castles of blue light
We've been here before

But which ocean is this?
The ocean of ignorance?

There's a reason we fear, fear
the lake, ocean, river, something greater

far greater than the self and all it contains
We may come from water but these cells
don't remember how to breathe—

breathe, pulse, shift, stone, blue, sound, ice
slow, move, lift, wave, eye, blue, sea
still, small, scared, we, *eight seven six*
stay, sleep, wake, hand, all and
child, love, love, lost

Breathe. These are the ways we are lost

~

We call it progress. This fragmenting. Cutting
ourselves
off

from the whole—constructing buildings like bulkheads
paving over the ground

sealing ourselves off
hermetically

So many kinds of heartbreak

The waters compassed me about and keep compassing
I am a needle   I am a pivoting sensing needle floating
swivelling   volte-face   the spirals   five
ocean gyres   things

                    fall

         apart

We keep letting them, spitting out particles
and refuse—how many years do you think it will take until—
how many overriding cannot-holds until—

~

Foolhardy to think anything is separate

~

And now they're siphoning carbon
straight from the air to slow the warming

As antidote, more plastic—
the world is shod with ironies

THE WORLD IS A GREAT WHINNYING HORSE RUNNING ROUGHSHOD

~

People always say look to those working to make it better

See me scouring the globe for teenage
inventors

great barriers (not reefs) to glean
our debris

Kenya, Samoa, Albania
Bangladesh

Montreal, Tofino, Chicago
LA

bamboo cutlery & dishes of banana leaves
biopolymers born of fish waste & algae

I look and look and still can't quite
tip over into hopeful

H. imagines drastic
action too. Becoming a warrior, running away

I'm sick now, my days are o-over

you can't always see it
microbeads flushing through our bloodstreams

I never want to look at the world and see only trash & shattering

someone needs to keep vigil keep valiant keep a *veille*

~

light
treetops catching light

winnowing shadow
river
river

never let this be obsolete

~

The whole world lifts for moments. The whole green world

Here now is the earth sounding singing

        I could drink it

earth stinking sweet stink mud leaf

       · mulch mint

trees breathing bending to the

        rivers sounding rolling wishing

bursting into seas o always & ever &

        these are the ways we are

found

   ~

"Something happened," says the boat builder,
"after el Niño": cyclones causing shifting seasons
and now beneath the golden bridge
the water's full and teeming

not just plastics—

krill, the water fills
the many in the one

and where the krill go, they follow

"Can you picture humpbacks breaching
under the Golden Gate?"

Went walking today thinking I'd head one way but my feet took me another. The world was dim. The park was dim. A hillside spilled with little white flowers. I ended up at the labyrinth. I tried to think of the right question. I stepped in and already water was surfacing. All of it so big and I can't not carry it. Walking ancient shapes—maybe this will help? Walking whorling paths—maybe something will unknot? There's a knot of sorrow so unfathomable in me. I want the story to take me somewhere.

But the book itself is a labyrinth and there's nowhere else to get to. No deliverance, no end.

A man passing called out, too loud, "You'll never escape!"

—

And of course
I got it wrong

My mother was nine when it happened. I was ten
when she told me. Old enough

to have an antenna out and
the telling was so careful, so hard won

My turn to form words like an inchworm
flailing

I didn't mean...
I didn't mean to...

The first time as an adult I heard her speak of it
to someone else, I cried and cried
Oh little her, oh little mother

How could I, how can I, go back now?
Stand guard with my sword where it counts?

—

I dream of a land at the edge of the ocean

wide white islands
moss and lichen

I soared like a lone
bird. I grew filled with starkness, with

the unseen
deeply alive

I could stand at the edge of a ridge and let my hair tangle in the wind
but really I was
formless

I was a breeze or the eyes
of a bird, the sight of a bird

Rooted in something spreading and wild

Words don't touch what I mean

Rooted is not it, at all

If there is reckoning to be done, the time has come. I send the manuscript to the boat builder.

He texts back: *I have read your book. There is nothing I would change, only details I might add. Keith Jarett needed an unplayable piano to record the best record of all time. Creativity's best comes when one is pushed into uncharted waters, where the abyss awaits. Though it may be cold you just dive right in.*

———

In the centre of the labyrinth
I place my hands on the stone, say
I give back what is not mine

I am not only that which I see but I hold all of it

———

Suddenly I am like a sky

something boundless and wild
watching over the earth

borderless, fluid

(Is this what I meant by something greater?)

I have the pages up on the wall, now, as I near the end

My mother comes over bearing gifts she's fermented
plants she has tended

She sits down inside the book with me

Just a person, tender

⁓

Hope? Hope is like a question mark in the deepest of the dark

Humpbacks have been seen again
from Manhattan—

⁓

Cetaceans swim by, holding our entire
reality in one eye and room for a whole other

moon tugging on different seas in the other

⁓

Hydrophones under arctic ice

twelve new songs

I have an image of the child
looking out through the adult's eyes

I see the one within
another

I see the small body
white fear dark joy

inside the blue wave
of the grown person

I turned off the lights
at the top of the stairs stepped down into silky dark

I looked through the peephole
of the furnace saw flames

I invented a game

the sun was always hasty and blaring

I went to the far end of the garden
wending on and on to the farthest back fence

and everywhere I went her sadness reached me

but it's getting late I can't
blame anyone
anymore

I'm suddenly overcome. We have so much
to grieve, so much to be grateful for, the wild
joys and arrows of life, this thing living us
through and through. We have to go through it
all of it

water weaving across this salty earth
this tough and vining earth
with creatures ready
only to behold. Asking
nothing

I'm tender now, tender and wet, breathing
air that flows through us, everyone. Hours
stream out leaving me here and holding my own head
my eyes, I was built to see everything
to love and let it go

I have loved bigger than my own bones

I know sadness but this
is new, a wide, embracing
mycelial sorrow
not racing to hide
not hiding

That pressing at my throat
Our sad, gorgeous earth

From here I slip
into the soft churning of clouds
slow and luminous
shadows of water
we are made of water

Compassing about my years, when years
were eons, when hours
stretched idle and long
across the distance
to my grandparents' house

I have walked through the cathedral of the whale

—

Eye for an eye for an eye
larger than any you've seen and wise

Sirius the Dog Star sees the whale seeing
you

Notes

p. 13 Discussion of improvisation in music and particularly the question of "how can you trick yourself into playing something new?" is informed by my conversation with performer-composer Dani Oore in 2009.

p. 35 "…dark movements of the moon / and of transparent, overlapping selves" is informed by Vicente Aleixandre's *The Longing for the Light*, edited by Lewis Hyde and translated by Hyde and fourteen other translators.

p. 35 "I thought I was free" is my translation of the line "Je croyais que j'étais libre" from the documentary by Laurent Esnault and Réjane Varrod.

p. 35 "Don't ask me who I am, or tell me to stay the same" is from *The Archaeology of Knowledge and the Discourse on Language*, 1972, Michel Foucault, translated by A.M. Sheridan Smith.

p. 51 *"tu devrais laisser le soleil te caresser le vent t'embrasser"* is my translation of words the boat builder remembers another boy telling him soon after his arrival to the boat.

p. 58 The phrase "If it feels good, it can't be hurting you. / Right?" is my translation of the quote from Kameneff *"Si je te fais du bien, c'est que je ne te fais pas de mal"* from the article entitled "Le procès exemplaire de l'École en bateau" in *Le Monde*, March 23, 2013.

pp. 59–62 The images of flying fish landing on the deck, boatloads full of bananas, a chisel slipping and a boy putting on Fauré in the morning are all drawn from Benoît Klam's book *Les perles de lumière*, as is the phrase *"pas comme ça qu'on commence le matin."*

p. 65 "sagittal slice" is from my translation of Maylis de Kerangal's novel *Mend the Living*.

pp. 68–73 anecdotal references to Foucault are drawn from *Michel Foucault* by Sara Mills and from *Foucault: A Graphic Guide* by Christopher Horrocks & Zoran Jetvic. The village simpleton story is called "The Story of Jouy," found in *The History of Sexuality Vol. 1* (& *L'Histoire de la Sexualité vol. 1*), which is also where all direct quotes are taken from.

p. 69 the "womb-cave" is informed by discussions about symbolism in Michel Tournier's *Friday or the Other Island*.

p. 87 "a thin / skin of water flowing endlessly" is borrowed from John Berger's line "a stone over which a skin of water flowed continuously" in *And Our Faces, My Heart, Brief as Photos*.

p. 88 "a word that comes in a good way" is influenced by the writings and oral storytelling of Leanne Betasamosake Simpson, in particular the concept of *mino bimaadiziwiin*.

p. 89 the concept "the future is dark and the best thing it can be" is from the diaries of Virginia Woolf.

pp. 91–95 The quotes from Kameneff in the section entitled "In his own words" are from the following sources: *Écoliers sans tabliers* by L. Kameneff; "École en bateau : Kameneff condamné à 12 ans de prison," *Le Figaro*, March 22, 2013; "L'affaire de pédophilie de l'École en bateau aux assises," *Le Figaro*, March 4, 2013; "Le Fondateur de l'école en bateau admet un 'jeu' sexuel," *Le Figaro*, March 6, 2013; "Procès de l'École en bateau: les aveux du fondateur," *Le Figaro*, March 15, 2013; "Les rêve brisées des moussaillons de l'École en bateau," *Le Parisien*, March 5, 2013. All translations are mine.

pp. 98, 108, 112 "je m'imaginais nager avec les baleines" is a slight alteration of the line "*je m'imaginais nager avec les dauphins*" (I imagined that I was swimming with the dolphins), as spoken by one of the former pupils of the *École* in the documentary by Laurent Esnault and Réjane Varrod.

p. 135 The notion of sound as a bridge, a physical connection, is informed by Daniela Gesundheit's introduction to the musical performance *An Alphabet of Wrongdoing*, in which she wrote, "the sound waves that I generate with my voice literally vibrate your cells… This bridge of sound erases the perceived spaces between you and me. When we gather to share music… we are practicing our inextricability."

pp. 135–36 The whale sounds I heard in the gallery were field recordings by Bernie Krause, remixed by Cosmo Sheldrake at the Fondation Cartier in Paris in 2016.

p. 158 "The wolf is not a threat / not sent to eat you if you tell" is directly informed by conversations with Phil Hall and by his book *Trouble Sleeping*.

pp. 160–84 Discussion of binaries in the final section is informed by *The Marvelous Clouds* by John Durham Peters.

p. 161 The notion of whales returning to the ocean while everyone else evolved onto land are from a talk by Jeff Warren about whales on the CBC.

p. 166 "We thrive off absence like Eros" is informed by Anne Carson's *Eros the Bittersweet*.

p. 169 reference to carrier bags and the way we carry stories is informed by Ursula K. Le Guin ("The Carrier Bag Theory of Fiction") and the ragtag collection of selves by my own 2001 essay on Virginia Woolf's *Orlando*.

Photographs on pages 25, 54, 75, 86, 90, 100, 106, 133, 137, 145, 157 and 159 are by Jacques Oulé.

Photographs / images on pages 44, 67, 96 and 153 are from boxes in the boat builder's coach house. In the photograph on page 67, he is the boy waiting to dive in.

The photograph on page 115 was taken by me at the end of the dead-end street.

Acknowledgements

This book is made of shards, most of them true. To call it poetry is only one facet. It contains elements of non-fiction, memoir and investigative documenting. Specific stories (the boat builder's, the author of the book's and my mother's) are shared with permission.

Any other details about what happened on board or during the trial came to me either through my conversations and correspondence with the boat builder, through the book by Benoît Klam, or through articles and documentaries from around the time of the trial. Even while giving a poetic rendering, and except for an instance or two of amalgams (in my mother's story and my own), I have not wanted to amplify or invent while treating other people's true stories.

The largest part of the book was written in a fifteenth-century building on a Spanish hillside in 2015, although it began in 2012 and "ended" (for the first time) in 2017, just before my babies were born, and for a second time in 2020 in the midst of a pandemic. Books are long journeys with many people to thank.

My gratitude to Reg, the original boat builder, whose voice got inside my head—I love you like strawberry jam. Thanks and love to Rich, Quill, Jenn, Laura, Dylan and all the boat builders for summertimes with the organ on the porch.

Thank you to Heather Davis for first telling me about the islands of plastic, and to Benoît Klam for such a warm correspondence. Thanks to Daria Chernysheva and Madeleine Stratford, fellow translators, and to David Ciavatta and Nikola Pezić and Noah Kenneally (though none would call himself an expert) for help with Foucault. I'm grateful to Sage Hill, Banff, Hoa Nguyen and Oana Avasilichoai, respectively, for helping open new channels. Thank you to Sylvain Prudhomme for an eye on the French, and to Cosmo Sheldrake and Amélie Deschamps for things you didn't know you'd given.

Je tiens à remercier et à exprimer ma reconnaissance envers les anciens élèves de l'École en bateau qui ont osé en parler. À ceux qui ont eu le courage d'apporter leur témoignage toutes ces années plus tard, merci.

Noëlie, Michaela, Breanna, Ani, Jocelyn, Erin, the Artscape gang and the ladies of Malaga—thank you for inspiration and grounding along the way. My thanks to Jan, Jim and Neal for their support and for allowing me (and so many of us) this sacred relationship with their land. I am endlessly grateful to Jacques for the images, brioche, the lilacs and his friendship.

Thank you to the OAC and the TAC for their support, and to Silas and Amber and everyone at Nightwood for tending so beautifully to words.

To friends and mentors who read sections of the manuscript in earlier forms (or in the final, crucial moments)—thank you. Phil Hall, Kate Cayley and Alayna Munce, your comments were invaluable. Erin Robinsong, thank you for bringing the marvellous library to Spain and for your constant magic. Johanna Skibsrud, I am so very lucky to have you.

There are three people without whom this book would never have come into being. My humble thanks to Adrian McCullough, the boat builder, for sharing so generously with me and allowing me to accompany his own discovery of events, and for graciously accepting my own slant lens and untethered memory. To Degan Davis: thank you, infinitely, for your wide view, your patience, the rivers of encouragement, for giving me hours to write and taking hours to read, and for helping shepherd this to completion—no one but me knows this book better than you. And to my mother, Angela Moore: my deepest thanks. For the gardens, the hours, the healing, the honesty and ballast, and this love that underlies it all.

About the Author

Jessica Moore is an author and literary translator. Her first book, *Everything, now* (Brick Books, 2012), is a love letter to the dead and conversation with her translation of *Turkana Boy* (Talonbooks, 2012) by Jean-François Beauchemin, for which she won a PEN America Translation award. *Mend the Living* (Talonbooks, 2016), her translation of the novel by Maylis de Kerangal, was nominated for the 2016 Man Booker International Prize and won the UK's Wellcome Prize in 2017. She lives in Toronto near the shores of Lake Ontario, that inland sea.

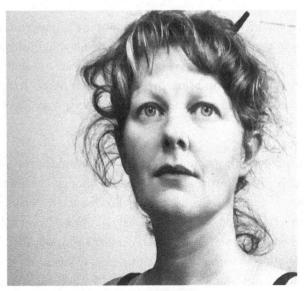

PHOTO CREDIT: ARLAN & SILAS DAVIS MOORE